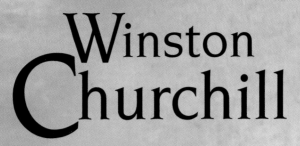

Winston Churchill

Katie Daynes

Designed by Karen Tomlins

History consultant: Terry Charman

Reading consultant: Alison Kelly

Edited by Jane Chisholm   Cover design by Russell Punter
Digital imaging Keith Furnival

First published in 2006 by Usborne Publishing Ltd., Usborne House,
83-85 Saffron Hill, London EC1N 8RT, England. www.usborne.com
Copyright © 2006 Usborne Publishing Ltd. The name Usborne and the
devices ♀⊕ are Trade Marks of Usborne Publishing Ltd.

ACKNOWLEDGEMENTS

© **Alamy** p13 (Popperfoto); © **British Library** p33; By permission of the Keepers and Governors
of Harrow School p8; © Centre for the Study of Cartoons and Caricature, University of Kent
p55 bottom; **Chartwell Booksellers** p30 bottom; © **CORBIS** front cover (Bettmann), back cover
(David Pollack), p1, pp2-3 (Bettmann), p6 (Bettmann), p11 (Hulton-Deutsch Collection), pp14-15
(Hulton-Deutsch Collection), 19 (Michael Maslan Historic Photographs), p24, pp28-29 (Colin
Garratt; Milepost 92½), p30 (Bettmann), p31 (Hulton-Deutsch Collection), p41 (Bettmann), p46
(Hulton-Deutsch Collection), p47 (Bettmann), pp48-49 (Bettmann), p49, p50 (Hulton-Deutsch
Collection), p51 (Bettmann), p52 (Bettmann), p55 left (David Pollack), p56 (Bettmann), p60, p61
(Bettmann), p64 (Bettmann); © **Getty Images** pp4-5 (David H Endersby), p16 (Time Life Pictures),
p22 (Time Life Pictures), p23, p27 (Time Life Pictures), p34, p53, pp58-59, p63; © **Harlan R.
Crow Library** p29; © **Illustrated London News** p10; © **MARY EVANS PICTURE LIBRARY** pp20-
21; **Supplied by Churchill Archives Centre, Cambridge, WHCL 5/18** p42; © **The Churchill
Heritage Ltd** p40 (reproduced with permission of Curtis Brown Ltd, London
on behalf of The Estate of Sir Winston Churchill); © **The National Trust** pp44-45;
© **TopFoto.co.uk** p7, p35, p43; © **Winston S. Churchill** p9 (reproduced with permission of
Curtis Brown Ltd, London on behalf of The Estate of Sir Winston Churchill);
With permission from IWM p25, pp36-37, pp38-39, p57
Every effort has been made to trace and acknowledge ownership of copyright.
The publishers offer to rectify any omissions in future
editions, following notification.

Contents

Winston Churchill meets
British troops during the
Second World War, 1944.

This is Blenheim Palace, where Winston
Churchill was born and his grandparents lived.

Internet links

You can find out more about Winston Churchill's fascinating
life by going to the Usborne Quicklinks Website at
www.usborne-quicklinks.com
and typing in the keyword **Churchill**.

At the Usborne Quicklinks Website you will find direct
links to a selection of recommended websites.
Here are a few of the things you can do:

- Listen to Churchill's famous speeches.
- See photographs of where he lived.
- Watch film footage from the Second World War.

The recommended websites are regularly reviewed and
updated but please note, Usborne Publishing is not
responsible for the content of any website other than its own.

Chapter 1

Finding his feet

Winston was a busy five-year-old with an army of toy soldiers to command. He was in the middle of a complex battle move, when he heard his nanny calling.

"Winston!" she cried. "Your governess has arrived."

"I must escape," thought Winston, quickly. He raced to the end of the garden and hid in the shrubbery. Two hours later, his hiding place was discovered and his dreaded education began.

Winston Churchill, aged five

Winston found lessons dreary and tiresome. Learning letters wasn't too bad. They joined together to make useful words. But numbers seemed to get tangled up in terrible knots.

"Nine nines are eighty-one, ten nines are... Oh really Winston, you'll be a laughing stock at boarding school," sighed his governess.

"Boarding school?" repeated Winston. The words filled him with fear. They meant leaving his soldier collection of over a thousand. Worse still, they meant leaving his nanny, Mrs. Everest, the most loving person in his life. Winston spent that afternoon sulking in his nursery.

6

"Mother and Father want to send me away," he sniffed. "I won't miss Father. He's so busy being a politician, I never see him anyway. I'll miss Mother's beautiful face. But how will I cope without my dear nanny."

There was a soft knock at the door and Mrs. Everest came in to comfort him. "We can write to each other," she promised. And they did.

From school, Winston wrote sorrowful letters about how he missed everyone, but only Mrs. Everest came to visit regularly. She was shocked by the beatings and bullying that took place. Eventually, she persuaded Winston's parents to move him to a more easy-going school by the sea.

Then, at the age of 12, Winston went to the highly rated senior school, Harrow.

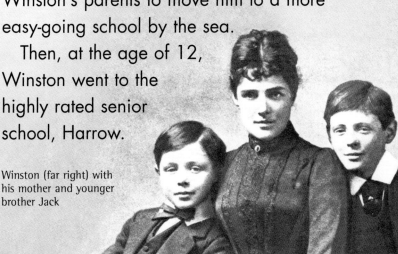

Winston (far right) with his mother and younger brother Jack

This photo shows Winston's house group at Harrow in 1892.
Winston is on the stairs, circled.

By now, Winston had grown taller and
more confident. He discovered that he hated
Latin even more than mathematics, but he
loved English and could memorize anything
if he put his mind to it. More importantly, he
knew how to have fun. Swimming, fencing,
eating and playing jokes on friends all
helped pass the days more quickly.

At the end of each term, Winston returned to Mrs. Everest's smiles and toy soldier battles with his younger brother Jack.

One summer, he had just forced Jack's troops to surrender when their father,

Doodles by Winston on a letter to his mother, 1887

Lord Randolph, burst into the nursery. Winston jumped to attention. His school reports had been even worse than usual and he dreaded what his father would say.

Lord Randolph paced back and forth, inspecting the tiny troops carefully positioned on the floor. Then he looked up at Winston. "Would you like to join the army?" he asked.

"Yes please!" blurted Winston. He loved the idea of commanding *real* troops.

And so, Winston's future career was chosen. Aged only 14, he joined the army class at school.

But getting into the army was much harder. After three years, Winston took the entrance exam to military training college and failed. He tried a second time... and failed again.

"We can't have you failing a *third* time," announced his father. "You must take intensive lessons. Captain James has a good crammer school in London."

Before Winston could meet the captain, he seriously injured himself in a game of chase. Standing on a bridge, Winston saw his brother at one end and his cousin at the other. The only way to avoid certain capture was to jump. It was further than Winston thought. He was unconscious for three days and bed-bound for three months.

Winston was taken to his father's London house to recover. It was a rare treat for a curious teenager. Mealtimes were often shared with Lord Randolph's colleagues – high-profile government ministers who eagerly discussed new policies and laws. Winston loved their witty chat and found their passion for politics catching.

As soon as he was well enough to walk, Winston went to hear a debate in the House of Commons. He peered down from the gallery at the MPs (Members of Parliament) below. They looked like soldiers, facing each other on the battlefield, only they used words to fight instead of weapons.

This is what the House of Commons looked like from the gallery in the 19th century.

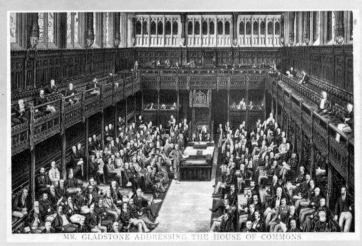

MR. GLADSTONE ADDRESSING THE HOUSE OF COMMONS

"When I'm not leading an army," thought Winston, "I want to be here, fighting for my people." But first he had to pass the army college entrance exam and, with Captain James' help, it was third time lucky.

Aged 19, Winston began his training at Sandhurst College and loved nearly every minute. Instead of Latin and mathematics, he was taught strategy and tactics. Days were filled drawing maps, digging trenches and making landmines. Best of all, Winston learned how to ride a horse. It quickly became a new passion. Winston and his cadet friends would spend all their spare time and money on horses and races.

The Royal Military College, Sandhurst, in the 1890s

When he graduated 15 months later, eighth out of 150 students, he knew the army was the right career for him. More specifically, he knew he wanted to fight on horseback.

"I'm joining a cavalry regiment," he told his parents.

"Please don't," pleaded his mother. "Horses are *so* expensive. Join the infantry instead."

Winston proudly poses in his Fourth Hussars uniform.

But Winston's stubborn mind was set... and he'd already been offered a job as an officer with the Fourth Hussars.

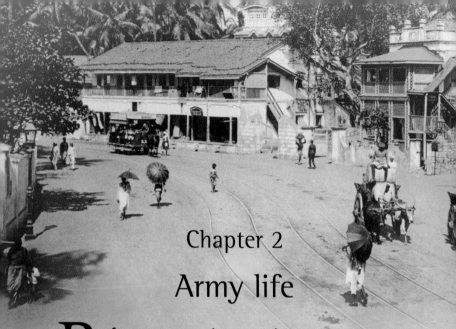

Chapter 2

Army life

Before joining the cavalry, Winston went to Cuba for an adventure. On his 21st birthday, he was delighted to witness real gunfire. The following year, he set sail for India with the Fourth Hussars. After a gruelling 23 day journey, dry land was a wonderful sight. In his eagerness to clamber ashore, Winston almost dislocated his shoulder. But he soon forgot the pain. Before him lay the exotic port of Bombay and the promise of adventures yet to come.

Life in the cavalry suited Winston well. His

This is how Bombay would have looked in 1896, when Winston arrived.

military duties began at dawn and were over by 11. For the middle part of the day, when the sun was at its fiercest, the regiment stayed inside resting, eating and sleeping.

Late afternoon was polo time. Nothing thrilled Winston more than charging on horseback, brandishing a stick and fighting over a small white ball. He would ignore his shoulder twinges and play on until sunset.

After a hot bath and dinner, Winston sat with his fellow officers, smoking in the moonlight. It was a civilized life, but Winston was an ambitious man and he soon felt restless. He thought of his school friends, now studying for university degrees in literature or law. "I need to improve my education," he decided.

Winston began to fill the hottest hours of the day reading and writing. His mother sent him all the history books he asked for. Then he moved onto books about politics. While other officers played cards or snoozed, Winston read up on the last 25 years of British government.

Winston in his early 20s

Aged 23, Winston was very well read and had visited many countries, but he still hadn't fought in a real battle. He was on leave in England, at the races, when he heard of a tribal revolt on the Indian border. Sir Bindon Blood was leading an army to fight the tribesmen.

"I must join them," thought Winston. He telegraphed Sir Bindon and, without waiting for a reply, set sail for the battle zone. At Bombay, he received Sir Bindon's response:

"Very difficult; no vacancies; come up as a correspondent; will try to fit you in. B.B."

Delighted, Winston began a five day train journey to the front line. Meanwhile, his mother was anxious about all the money her son was spending. She managed to strike a deal with the *Daily Telegraph* and, for £5* per column, Winston became their new war correspondent, reporting news directly from the front line.

*£5 in 1897 is equivalent to £370 today.

Over the next few months, Winston experienced the real action he had been waiting for. Danger, bravery and death were all around him. He came face to face with the enemy, lived to tell the tale and told it well. Along with newspaper columns, Winston produced an 85,000 word book about Blood's campaign. It was a huge success. Even the Prince of Wales wrote to congratulate him.

And so Winston's dual role as a reporter and officer began. When Sir Herbert Kitchener was planning a vast campaign in Sudan, Winston asked to be at the forefront of the action.

"No," came Kitchener's reply. He didn't want an ambitious reporter just coming along for the ride.

Winston's mother knew Kitchener quite well, but even a polite letter from her yielded no joy. He seemed destined to miss out on this war, until a remarkable stroke of luck.

The Prime Minister had just read Winston's book and wanted to meet its author. After a pleasant chat, Winston mentioned his desire to fight in the Sudan. A week later, thanks to the Prime Minister's influence, Winston was invited to join Kitchener's army.

He reached Egypt just in time to join the British troops. They journeyed by steamship down the River Nile, deeper and deeper into the African continent, then rode for days across the burning desert.

Winston would have sailed on a steamship similar to this one, photographed on the River Nile in 1900.

Eventually, through the shimmering heat, they spied their enemy – a long brown smear on the horizon. As they came closer, Kitchener lined up his men and gave the command, "Charge!"

Winston felt a rush of exhilaration as he galloped toward the enemy. Many men died that day, but the British and Egyptians were victorious. Lucky Winston returned without a scratch and was so inspired by the experience, he wrote another book.

A painting of the Sudan cavalry charge by war artist Edward Matthew Hale, 1898

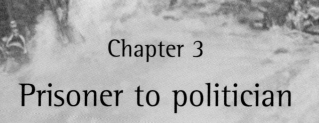

Chapter 3

Prisoner to politician

Winston's mother was right. Life in the cavalry *was* very expensive. His father, Lord Randolph, had died after a long illness, so Winston now received a yearly allowance. But this barely covered his polo expenses. Even with his extra money from writing, Winston began to fall into debt.

"I shall return to India and win the polo tournament," decided Winston. "Then I shall leave the army and concentrate on writing and politics."

Winston stands with one of his horses in India, 1896.

The tournament started badly. Four days before the first match, Winston fell on his weak shoulder. But the other players still picked him for the team and, with his elbow tightly strapped to his side, Winston scored the winning goal.

Saying fond farewells to the Fourth Hussars, he returned to England and his book on the Sudan. He lived at home with his mother and immersed himself in writing.

One day, he was invited to the House of

Commons. The Conservative party was looking for a new candidate to stand as an MP for Oldham town. Winston rose to the challenge. He made speeches in front of large crowds and argued for the Conservative government's policies.

In the end, a Liberal candidate won by 1,300 votes. Still, Winston's efforts weren't in vain. His enthusiasm and sparkling speeches had impressed many people and a pathway into politics was opening up.

But, before pursuing a new career, he was lured away by the opportunity to report on another war. Relations in South Africa between the British and the Dutch settlers, known as Boers, had reached crisis point.

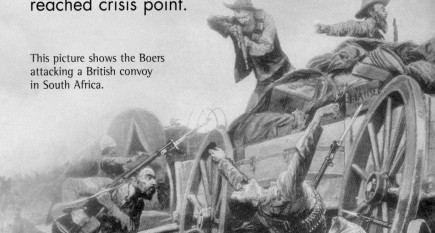

This picture shows the Boers attacking a British convoy in South Africa.

Even before war was declared, the *Morning Post* offered Winston a job as their principal war correspondent.

"We'll pay you £250* a month, plus expenses," said the editor.

Three days later, Winston was on a steamship headed

Winston the war correspondent in South Africa, 1899

for South Africa. By the time he arrived, the war was already in full swing and the Boers were forcing the British to retreat. Winston journeyed by train until his route was cut off. He joined the British troops waiting for reinforcements and met up with an old acquaintance, Captain Haldane.

"I'm taking an army train up the track,"

*£250 in 1899 is equivalent to £18,500 today.

the captain told him, "to see how close the enemy is. Would you care to join me?"

"Absolutely!" replied Winston.

They had journeyed 14 miles when the Boers sprang out and fired at them. The driver quickly reversed the train but, as they picked up speed, there was a tremendous jolt. Three of the carriages spun off the rails, killing many troops and injuring 40 others.

The train stopped dead. Within minutes, it was surrounded by menacing Boers. Winston peered out of the window.

Winston was in an army train like this one.

"There are toppled carriages blocking our way," he said, hurriedly. "We'll have to shunt them off the track."

"All right," said Captain Haldane. "Take some men and clear the way. We'll cover you."

Eventually, Winston freed the engine and one carriage. There was only enough room for the wounded men to crowd onboard. The others would have to follow on behind. As the train moved off, Winston raced back to help the captain.

Suddenly, he found himself face to face with two Boers. He dodged their bullets and fled, only to run into another armed Boer on horseback. Winston quickly reached for his pistol. It wasn't there. He was left with two choices, surrender or die.

Winston was captured, along with Haldane and his soldiers. They were taken on a long train journey to Pretoria prison.

Winston (right) and his fellow prisoners

Over the dreary weeks that followed, Winston, Haldane and a sergeant named Brockie plotted how to escape. They watched the guards' every move and scanned the prison walls for weak spots.

"That area is always in shadow," Winston whispered, pointing to the lavatory block. "We could make a dash for it when the guards aren't looking..."

27

Winston hid on a steam train carrying coal.

In the end, Winston escaped alone. He waited in the undergrowth for Haldane and Brockie. They never came. He was a free man, but he was 280 miles inside Boer territory.

With only four slabs of chocolate to eat, he needed to travel quickly. While it was still dark, he leaped onto a coal train and hid among the dusty sacks. He slept a little but, afraid of being caught, he jumped out before dawn.

When the Boers realized Winston had escaped, they offered £25 for his capture – dead or alive. Winston desperately needed food and help, but who could he trust?

The Boers issued a "wanted" poster for Winston Churchill and offered a reward of £25 (£1,850 today).

The following night, he reached a coal mine. Taking a huge risk, he crept up to the largest house and knocked. Minutes passed, then an Englishman, John Howard, opened the door... and came to Winston's rescue. He hid him down a mine shaft for three days, until the Boers' search party had moved off.

"The best way to the frontier is by train," said Howard. "We're going to hide you in a truck filled with wool. Here, take this pistol."

It was a stuffy, tense journey, lasting three long days. Fortunately, Winston had two roast chickens, a loaf of bread, a melon and three bottles of cold tea to keep him company.

He was scared to sleep in case he snored, and terrified of being found every time the train stopped. Finally he reached the safety of neutral territory.

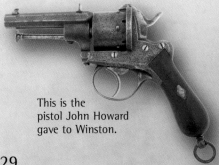

This is the pistol John Howard gave to Winston.

Winston in Durban, 1899,
a free man once more

That same evening, he boarded a ship to Durban where the British troops gave him a hero's welcome.

Accounts of Winston's adventures were eagerly followed in the British newspapers. He returned home to discover he was famous.

"You must stand as an MP again," said Lord Salisbury, the Prime Minister.

This time, enough people voted for Winston to make him a member of the British parliament. His life in politics had begun, though he still found time to write another book.

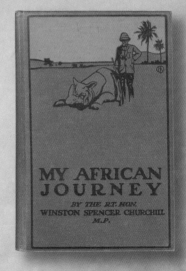

MY AFRICAN JOURNEY
BY THE RT. HON.
WINSTON SPENCER CHURCHILL
M.P.

This is Winston's book about his adventures in South Africa. It was first published in 1908.

Chapter 4

The Great War

Winston stayed in the Conservative party for four years. He had strong opinions and loved voicing them in public. But his views had more in common with the Liberals. When the Conservatives introduced several policies Winston didn't like, he decided it was time to change parties. It was a wise move. Two years later, the Liberals won the general election.

Winston, now a Liberal MP, makes a speech to crowds in Manchester.

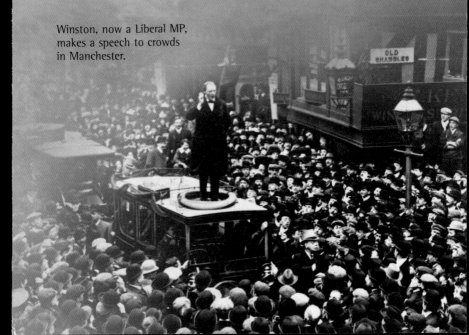

Politics, reading and riding took up most of Winston's time, but there were also endless social engagements. He enjoyed good food and fine wines but he hated dancing and found polite chatter very dull. The only topics of conversation that excited him were himself and the future of the world.

"We are all worms," he told one young lady over dinner. "But I do believe that I am a glow worm."

Aged 33, Winston was attending yet another dinner party when he found himself next to a beautiful young woman. Her name was Clementine and Winston thought she was wonderful. He spent the evening talking animatedly, hoping to charm her with his long words and funny stories.

Clementine was fascinated by the lively politician. He wrote to her and she wrote back. The first letters were formal and awkward, but gradually the couple grew bolder and confessed their love. Within six months, Winston proposed and Clementine accepted. They married the very next month.

Winston and Clementine's wedding, as reported in the *Daily Graphic*, 1908

The newlyweds spent their honeymoon in Italy, then moved to a house in London. Within three years they had two children, Diana and Randolph, and Winston had an exciting new job. The Prime Minister had appointed him First Lord of the Admiralty – head of the British navy. With the job came a large house and a huge yacht. Winston spent most weekends sailing from port to port, checking up on his warships.

Winston inspects boys training to be sailors, 1912.

Winston spends a rare moment
with his wife and son, in 1912.

On the rare days he wasn't working, he
joined Clementine and the children on family
outings. He loved sunny afternoons at the
seaside, when he could wallow in the warm
water and sprawl out on the hot sand.

Meanwhile, the British government was
receiving worrying reports from across the
sea. The German emperor was rapidly
increasing his fleet.

"He's building three battleships a year,"
Winston told the Admiralty. "That means we
must build *four*."

On August 4th, 1914, German troops invaded Belgium. The British government issued an ultimatum – withdraw by midnight or face war with Britain.

When the Germans refused to leave, Winston spun into action. He sent his new ships to track down the enemy. But luck wasn't always with the British navy. In just one day the Germans sank three British cruisers, killing 1,400 sailors.

Winston felt frustrated stuck in London. He wanted to be fighting alongside his men. When Kitchener needed someone for an army mission to Flanders in Belgium, Winston volunteered himself.

"He's neglecting the navy," murmured government ministers.

"He's neglecting me," thought Clementine. While Winston was rallying troops in Belgium, she was giving birth to their third child, Sarah.

Winston was appalled by the number of British soldiers dying on the front line. They lived in water-logged, rat-ridden trenches. Every time they tried to attack the Germans, hundreds of them were shot down.

"Why are we sending our armies to chew barbed wire in Flanders?" Winston asked his colleagues.

British troops in the trenches, 1918

He was sure that a sea attack would be more effective. By now, Turkey was fighting on Germany's side, so Winston decided to send his navy along the Turkish coast, to an area known as the Dardanelles. He hoped that British ships would intimidate Turkey, and that a show of strength might persuade other countries to join the war against the Germans.

Admiral Fisher, working with Winston, strongly disagreed with attacking the Dardanelles. "They'll be our grave!" he argued. But Winston wouldn't listen.

As the campaign whirled out of control, Winston grew more stubborn and Fisher

began to despair. Thousands of soldiers were stranded on the hostile Turkish coast, in easy reach of the Turkish army. Many of them were killed or injured.

While Winston looked for reinforcements, Fisher wrote a letter of resignation. "I am unable to remain any longer as your colleague," he stated. "I am off to Scotland at once to avoid all questionings."

Shortly afterwards, Winston was removed as First Lord of the Admiralty and given a minor role in the war council instead. He felt wounded by the demotion and grew increasingly depressed.

This rare and faded photograph, taken in 1915, shows hundreds of troops from Britain, Australia and New Zealand trapped between the sea and the rocky Turkish cliffs.

"I am finished!" he sighed to a friend over drinks late one night. "Finished in respect of all I care for – the waging of war, the defeat of the Germans..."

That summer, he hid away in a rented farmhouse outside London. His brother's wife Gwendoline, nicknamed Goonie, came to visit and encouraged Winston to take up painting. For hours at a time, he became completely absorbed in his new hobby.

"It's a miracle!" Clementine exclaimed to Goonie. "Finally we've found something that calms Winston down."

This painting from 1915 is one of Winston's first.

But Winston didn't stay calm for long. Determined to help defeat the Germans, he resigned from the government and asked to fight in the trenches. "I am an officer," he wrote to the Prime Minister. "I place myself unreservedly at the disposal of the military authorities."

A week later, Winston – now Major Churchill – joined British troops in France. He was thrilled to be under enemy fire again.

Winston in his army uniform, 1916

"They all say I look five years younger," he wrote to his wife. He avoided worrying her with details of the everyday dangers. Instead, he asked for packages of chocolate, sardines and brandy.

Within six weeks, Winston was promoted to lieutenant-colonel and given his own battalion to command.

Winston, circled, with his battalion in France, 1916

He had two weeks to prepare his troops
for the trenches, so he started a rigorous
training routine of football and singing.
The men respected their new colonel and
their spirits were high. But, once the
battalion had settled into trench life, Winston
began to feel restless again. He missed
being in government, shaping the future of
Britain. He also missed his wife.

"We are still young," he read in one of
her many letters, "but time flies, stealing
love away and leaving only friendship."

Winston decided he must return home. He
left the army after only six months and spent

the remainder of the war as Minister of Munitions, in charge of British weapon supplies. It should have meant more time in London with his family, but he couldn't resist regular trips to France to check the front line.

On November 11th, 1918, the Germans finally admitted defeat and the war was over. Winston stood at his office window watching the crowds celebrate across the streets of London. He was pleased but not elated. What cause was he going to fight for now?

People celebrate the end of the war on board a London bus, November 11th, 1918.

Chapter 5
Peacetime

While the government busied itself with peacetime politics, Winston looked for a new project. He fell in love with Chartwell, a run-down old manor in the countryside. It had acres of gardens and a fantastic view. Winston was determined to buy it.

Clementine begged him not to. "It'll take years to renovate and will cost us a fortune," she sighed. "And we'll be so far from friends in London."

Her arguments silenced Winston and he pretended to give

up on the idea. But months later, on the day that Clementine gave birth to their daughter Mary, he made a secret offer on the house.

When Winston finally told his wife, she was furious. "How could you!" she cried. "You must withdraw your offer immediately."

"Too late," he confessed. "It's already been accepted."

That year, Winston failed to get re-elected as an MP. It was a blow to his political career, but it gave him time to work on his beloved Chartwell.

Chartwell was Winston's home from 1924 until he died.

He redesigned the main building, dammed the river and built his own brick walls in the garden. The new house was a perfect place to write and Winston soon plunged himself into another book: *World Crisis*, a history of the First World War.

Clementine was still angry about Chartwell. While her husband insisted on spending every moment there, she organized lots of trips overseas, visiting friends and family, and often leaving Winston to take care of their four children.

Winston wasn't worried by her absence. He had set his sights on becoming an MP again, this time back with the Conservatives. He found their new policies appealing and, after meeting the right people, he stood as one of their candidates in the next election. Winston was delighted to be

Winston loved bricklaying. He even became an honorary member of the local Bricklaying Union.

Winston as
Chancellor of
the Exchequer
in 1929

voted in and overwhelmed when the new
Prime Minister asked him to be Chancellor
of the Exchequer.

For the next five years, he was in charge
of the country's money. With the job came a
spacious London house – 11 Downing Street.
Clementine was thrilled, but Winston still
loved escaping to Chartwell.

When the Conservatives lost the next
election, Winston remained an MP but no
longer had a government role. Instead, he
returned to writing books and mulling over
the state of the world. It concerned him to
see Germany becoming more powerful.

In 1914, he had feared the mighty German navy. Twenty years later, he felt their air force posed a greater threat... and he told the British parliament so.

"An air attack would expose us not only to hideous suffering," he warned, "but even to mortal peril."

Most MPs thought Winston was making a big fuss over nothing.

"It's the Dardanelles all over again," jeered one Liberal.

"The old man has lost his marbles," mocked another.

By now, Winston had reached the grand age of 60. Many thought his

political career was over. But Winston ignored them. He knew he was right to speak out against Germany.

In the last few years, the German Nazi party had risen to power, led by Adolf Hitler. Winston was alarmed by Hitler's aggressive new policies, and appalled by his treatment of Jews.

He complained endlessly to his wife. "How can Hitler hate someone just because they're Jewish?" he ranted. "That man's going to cause trouble... and no one in Europe has the guts to stop him."

Nazi soldiers gather for their annual rally at Nuremberg, Germany. In the foreground, Adolf Hitler makes his infamous salute.

Before long, Hitler marched his troops into the Rhineland, then took over Austria. Winston urged the British government to take immediate action, but the Prime Minister, Neville Chamberlain, was desperate to avoid another war with Germany.

When Hitler plotted to take over Czechoslovakia, Chamberlain flew to Germany to dissuade him. Instead, he ended up agreeing to Hitler's demands.

"I am a man of peace to the depths of my soul," Chamberlain later explained on British radio. He thought Hitler would be satisfied now, but he was wrong.

Chamberlain and Hitler discuss Czechoslovakia's future over tea in Munich, 1938.

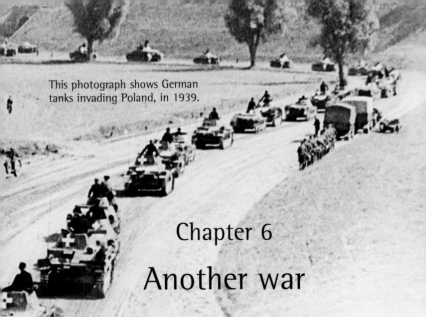

This photograph shows German tanks invading Poland, in 1939.

Chapter 6

Another war

On September 1st, 1939, Germany invaded Poland. Chamberlain solemnly announced the news to parliament.

"Well, there's a surprise," muttered Winston from his back bench.

"It now only remains for us to set our teeth," Chamberlain went on, "and to enter upon this struggle..."

"And about time too!" thought Winston. Finally, Chamberlain had accepted that Hitler was evil and needed to be stopped.

Chamberlain set up a war cabinet and invited Winston to be a member. Then he offered Winston his old job, First Lord of the Admiralty. Winston accepted graciously. It had been ten long years since he last held a position in government. Now he had a chance to make a real difference.

He returned to Admiralty House with renewed energy. Within hours, Britain officially declared war with Germany and there was lots of work to do. Winston began a series of radio broadcasts on the war.

Winston summarizes the first month of the war in a radio broadcast to the British people, 1939.

People gather in a London pub to listen to Winston on the radio.

He didn't just tell the public about naval news. He reviewed the entire war situation, even asking other nations to join forces with Britain. "The day will come when the joy-bells will ring again throughout Europe..." he proclaimed.

The public loved hearing his positive messages, but Winston's words covered up a stark truth. Britain was losing men and ships, while Germany grew stronger.

Meanwhile, politicians were grumbling about the way the war was going. They thought the government was doing a poor job and they blamed Chamberlain.

"You've sat too long here for any good you've been doing," called out a Conservative MP.

Winston was quick to own up to any mistakes made by the Admiralty, but no one seemed to blame him. Politicians from both sides wanted Chamberlain to go, and they wanted someone more dynamic to take over.

The two most likely candidates were Lord Halifax and Winston Churchill. Chamberlain invited them both to tea.

"It wouldn't be right for a lord to be Prime Minister," sighed Lord Halifax.

"Nonsense," replied Chamberlain.

For once, Winston kept very quiet.

When Chamberlain realized Halifax was past persuading, he turned to Winston. "Then the job's yours," he said, reluctantly.

The next day, Chamberlain went to Buckingham Palace, offered his resignation to the King and advised him to send for Winston Churchill.

It was a wonderful moment for Winston. At the age of 65, he was finally about to lead his country.

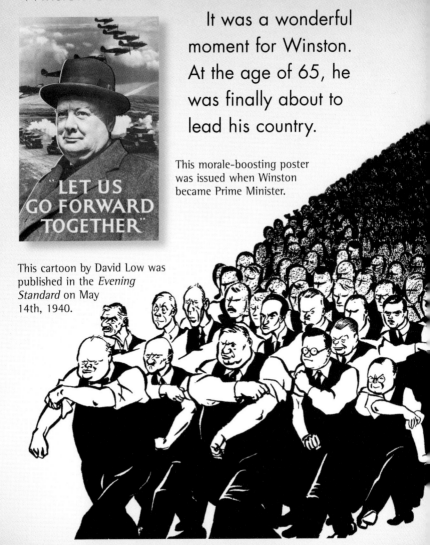

This morale-boosting poster was issued when Winston became Prime Minister.

This cartoon by David Low was published in the *Evening Standard* on May 14th, 1940.

"LET US GO FORWARD TOGETHER"

All Behind You, Winston

"I have nothing to offer but blood, toil, tears and sweat," he announced in his first speech. It felt as if all his life had been leading up to this moment. He would be a voice of conviction in a time of crisis, and the nation would love him for it.

But when Winston was away from parliament and his people, his mood turned gloomy. "I hope it's not too late," he sighed.

Winston meets the French leader, Charles de Gaulle.

During the weeks and months that followed, Winston was frantically busy. He made five trips to France, to boost morale and urge the French not to surrender.

When German tanks forced their way into France, British and French troops risked being cut off. So Winston ordered their immediate evacuation.

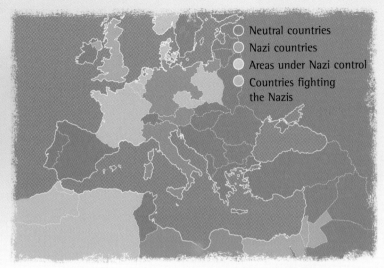

This is a map of Europe in July 1940, when Poland, Norway, Denmark, Holland, Belgium and France were all under Nazi control.

Neutral countries
Nazi countries
Areas under Nazi control
Countries fighting the Nazis

It was his first major triumph. Over 300,000 troops were successfully rescued and brought back to England.

Troops wait for rescue ships on the beaches at Dunkirk in France, 1940.

Soon, Hitler's fearless army reached the French coast and there was only a narrow stretch of sea between them and Britain. Winston had to keep his nation believing that victory was still possible.

"We shall defend our island," he declared in parliament. "We shall fight on the beaches... we shall fight in the fields and in the streets, we shall fight in the hills; we shall never surrender."

His words may have been full of hope, but the outlook was getting bleaker. As other European countries surrendered to the Nazis, Britain became increasingly isolated.

And then the bombs began to fall.

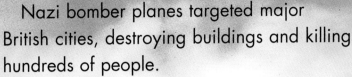

Nazi bomber planes targeted major British cities, destroying buildings and killing hundreds of people.

"We cannot continue to fight alone," thought Winston, gloomily. He desperately wanted help from Russia and America, but they were reluctant to get involved in someone else's war. As the number of deaths continued to mount, even Winston found it hard to sound positive.

St Paul's cathedral towers over the bomb damage in central London.

Then, within a year, everything changed. Hitler invaded Russia, and the Japanese – eager to expand their empire in Asia – attacked the American navy. The Russian leader, Stalin, and the American President, Roosevelt, had little choice but to join the war against Nazi Germany.

Left to right: Stalin, Roosevelt and Churchill, meeting in 1943

Winston spent the long months that followed journeying from one country to the next, talking tactics and rallying support. Unfortunately, the pressures of the job put great strain on his health and meant he hardly ever saw his family. Many orders or speeches he dictated from his bed, and sometimes even his bath. But he always found the energy to rise for important occasions.

For months, Britain and America had been planning a massive attack on the French beaches. Their troops would arrive by sea and air, and a mixture of surprise and numbers would force the Nazis to retreat.

"I'll be there, on the first ship," said Winston to his colleagues. They hoped he was joking, but a mischievous look in his eye told them otherwise.

Only the king could persuade Winston not to lead the attack. Instead, he visited the beaches six days later. He was relieved to see the troops making good progress. The tide had turned on the Nazis and, at last, victory was in sight.

American troops arrive on the French coast.

Chapter 7

A ripe old age

On 8th May, 1945, Winston addressed the British people and announced victory in Europe.

"Now you can retire," said Clementine, hopefully. "We could move to Chartwell..."

"Retire?" blurted Winston. "Not likely!"

His wife worried that victory had gone to his head. "Darling, people want to put the war behind them," she urged. "They want a change of government."

Winston didn't listen, so defeat at the next election came as a real blow. But still he didn't retire. He remained leader of the Conservatives and four years later, aged 77, he was re-elected as Prime Minister.

He suffered a stroke and made a remarkable recovery. In 1953 he won the Nobel Prize for Literature. Then his wife made him promise to retire after his 80th birthday, and he did. The rest of his life he spent writing, painting and going abroad.

Finally, at the ripe old age of 90, he suffered a massive stroke and died. People came from all over the world to pay their respects to this remarkable man.

Winston's funeral procession snakes its way through London, 1965.

My place in history

1874 – I was born at Blenheim Palace.

1882 – I'm sent away to a horrible boarding school.

1884 – I move to a friendlier school by the sea.

1888 – I start at Harrow public school.

1889 – I join the army class.

1893 – I finally pass my entrance exam for Sandhurst.

1895 – My father, Lord Randolph, dies. I spend my
21st birthday under fire in Cuba.

1896 – I sail to India with the Fourth Hussars.

1898 – I join Kitchener's army in Sudan.

1899 – I go to South Africa to report on the
Boer war. I am captured... and escape!

1900 – Back in England, I am elected MP for Oldham.

1904 – I switch from the Conservatives to the Liberals.

1908 – I propose to my dearest Clementine and we
get married the following month.

1909 – Our first child, Diana, is born.

1911 – Our son Randolph is born and I am appointed
First Lord of the Admiralty.

1914 – The First World War begins. Our daughter Sarah is born.

1915 – The failure of the Dardanelles campaign
loses me my job. I learn to paint
before joining the troops.

1917 – I am appointed Minister of Munitions.

1921 – My darling mother dies.

1924 – I switch back to the Conservatives and become
Chancellor of the Exchequer.

1939 – We are at war with Nazi Germany and I am
First Lord of the Admiralty again.

1940 – I become Prime Minister. The evacuation at
Dunkirk is my first success.

1944 – We celebrate victory in Europe.

1945 – The world is at peace and the
Conservatives are voted out of office.

1951 – I become Prime Minister once again!

1955 – I retire, aged 80, and concentrate on painting.

Winston S. Churchill